THE
LAW OF
PASSING-OFF

BY

CHRISTOPHER WADLOW

SOLICITOR
SIMMONS & SIMMONS
LONDON

FIRST SUPPLEMENT TO THE
SECOND EDITION

LONDON
SWEET & MAXWELL
1997

Published in 1997 by
Sweet & Maxwell Limited of
100 Avenue Road, London NW3 3PF
Computerset by Interactive Sciences, Gloucester
Printed and bound in Great Britain
by Headway Press, Reading

No natural forests were destroyed to
make this product: only farmed timber
was used and replanted.

ISBN 0 421 594209
A CIP catalogue record for this book is
available from the British Library

CONTENTS

GENERAL NOTE

This Supplement contains material which has become available in the two years since August 1994 when the text of the main work was finalised, including a number of currently unreported cases of which the most important is *Harrods v. Harrodian School* in the Court of Appeal.[1] Now that *The Law of Passing-Off* is part of Sweet & Maxwell's *Intellectual Property Library* it is my intention to prepare future supplements at approximately two-yearly intervals until publication of the next edition.

Each entry in the Supplement has a marginal reference in the bold type to the paragraph of the Main Work to which it relates, identified by headings and sub-headings corresponding to those in the Main Work.

Cross references within the text of the Supplement relate to other supplementary paragraphs within the Supplement, unless otherwise stated.

This Supplement also contains supplementary Tables of Cases, Statutes, European Treaties and Conventions and Rules of the Supreme Court, as well as a supplementary Index, each of which is to be read in conjunction with the corresponding Table or Index in the Main Work, each against the paragraph number quoted therein.

[1] Court of Appeal, April 2, 1996, to be reported.

TABLE OF CASES

TABLE OF STATUTES

TABLE OF STATUTORY INSTRUMENTS

TABLE OF RULES OF THE SUPREME COURT

GOODWILL

A. THE IMPORTANCE OF GOODWILL

Distinction with trade mark rights

2.03   The majority judgments of the Court of Appeal in *Harrods v. Harrodian School*[1] emphasise that even a name which could be described as "world-famous" and "a household name" is not protected in its own right: the defendants were free to use the adjectival form as the name of their school, because the goodwill of the plaintiffs in their business of a department store did not stand to be damaged.[2]

Distinction between goodwill and reputation

2.08   The plaintiffs' argument in *Harrods v. Harrodian School*[3] that the reputation of *Harrods* would suffer because of an alleged adulterous affair between the Headmistress and the English Master at the defendant school reminds one that *Harrods* has prospered over a decade in which it has been at the centre of litigation in which far more serious allegations have been traded. In one of these cases, the Court of Appeal dealt with an action for conspiracy to injure by lawful means (in which pecuniary damage is the gist of the action) with Dillon L.J. observing[4]:

> "To prove loss of orders and loss of trade is another matter; that is recognisable pecuniary damage. . . . Such loss of orders, for example, would involve injury to the goodwill of a business which may be one of the most important assets of the business. But goodwill in that sense must have the meaning put on that word in *Trego v. Hunt* [1896] A.C. 7: see especially, per Lord Herschell, at pp. 17–18, and per Lord Macnaghten, at p. 24. It cannot mean some airy-fairy general reputation in the business or commercial community which is unrelated to the buying and selling or dealing with customers which is the essence of the business of any trading company."

B. THE MEANING OF "BUSINESS" AND "TRADER"

The boundaries of trading activity

2.12   The judgment of Walker J. in *British Diabetic Association v. The Diabetic Society*[5] illustrates that there is no completely satisfactory policy answer to

---

[1] Court of Appeal, to be reported.

[2] Though the status of *Harrods* as a household name lessened, but did not eliminate, the significance of the absence of any common field of activity, according to Millett L.J.

[3] *Supra.*

[4] *Lonrho plc v. Fayed and others (no. 5)* [1993] 1 W.L.R. 1489, C.A. On an application to strike out, the damage which allowed the re-amended statement of claim to stand was to Lonrho's various trading interests. Claims by Lonrho and individual plaintiffs for conspiracy to damage their reputation were struck out as sounding in defamation or not at all.

[5] [1996] F.S.R. 1 (Robert Walker J.).

whether one charity (etc.) should be able to sue another for passing-off. An action between two charities properly so called was "on the face of it . . . a deplorable, even a scandalous thing" because funds intended for charitable purposes were diverted into litigation. An exception would be an action against a so-called charity which was really "a sham or a scam . . . a bogus charity . . . diverting funds from an established and properly-run charity in circumstances amounting to passing-off" but in the instant case there was no allegation that the individual defendants were motivated by private gain. None the less, the judge accepted that an action for passing-off lay in principle and granted a permanent injunction. The plaintiff charity had a trading subsidiary but this was not relevant to the decision. What was more relevant was that the plaintiff charity was, perhaps unusually, one where both benefactors and beneficiaries were largely drawn from the same class of the population and to that extent had some of the character of a self-help association. It would probably be wrong, however, to suppose that charities such as the NSPCC or RNLI (the examples given by the judge) would fail in otherwise comparable circumstances.

Nice and Safe Attitude v. Flook[6] is inconclusive as to whether the scientific activities of the American National Aeronautics and Space Administration (NASA) were relevant to passing-off, since it had little presence in England and in any event they were too remote from the field of fashion clothing. A licence from NASA (USA) to the defendant's suppliers did not avail the defendant against a plaintiff who had actually used *NASA* for clothing.

Trade and professional associations

Examples

The Law Society has been a successful plaintiff in two recent cases. In *Law* **2.14** *Society v. Griffiths*[7] the plaintiffs were awarded an interlocutory injunction to protect the freephone number of their "Accident Line" referral service against the use of a similar number by the defendant firm of solicitors. Not only would member firms of the plaintiffs' scheme lose business, but confidence in the scheme would be undermined and member firms would become disaffected with it. In *Law Society v. Society of Lawyers*[8] the defendants were in reality a commercial organisation which purported to offer membership, for a fee,[9] to persons (not necessarily individuals) who were not necessarily lawyers properly so-called but who might have various quasi-legal qualifications or practical experience. Membership criteria were so lax as to be a sham, certain individuals in important positions were unfit to exercise their purported roles and the defendant Society did not exercise any of the normal functions of a bona fide professional association. Rimer J. granted the Law Society an interlocutory injunction.

[6] (Robert Walker J., February 8, 1996).
[7] [1995] R.P.C. 16 (Aldous J.).
[8] [1996] F.S.R. 739 (Rimer J.).
[9] A larger fee bought the right to call oneself an Area Secretary and receive a commission on new members recruited.

The plaintiffs in *Scotch Whisky Association v. J. D. Vintners*[10] sued for passing-off and breach of Community law[11] by the sale of a spirit as "Light Canadian Rye." This had a strength of 30 per cent alcohol, compared to a minimum strength of 40 per cent for whisky. It was alleged that the name "Light Canadian Rye" implicitly misrepresented the product as whisky properly so called. The first plaintiff was a trade association suing in its personal, rather than representative, capacity. The two other plaintiffs were whisky distillers and blenders. On an application to strike out part of the statement of claim Scott V.-C. agreed that the first plaintiff had no cause of action in passing-off, distinguishing a number of cases where the *locus standi* of similar trade associations had not been challenged:

> "It is, as I understand it, accepted by the plaintiff that the Association does not have a cause of action in passing off. If that is accepted, it is, in my opinion, rightly accepted. I cannot see on what basis a trade association can maintain a passing off action based upon conduct which constitutes a passing off by the defendant of its products for those of the members of the trade association. The trade association, if it sues in a representative capacity, can perhaps maintain such an action but that would be to base the action on the combined causes of action of its members. Such an action would not be based upon a cause of action vested in the Association itself."

Associations: the rationale for protection

2.15   *Law Society v. Griffiths*[12] seems to align itself with *BMA v. Marsh*[13] in its reasoning. The latter case was not referred to expressly by Aldous J., but it is of interest that he focused on the Society's activities in running a personal injuries panel and referral service rather than on its functions in general. In *Law Society v. Society of Lawyers*[14] Rimer J. was rather more troubled with the *locus standi* of the plaintiffs but held that they had at least an arguable case.[15]

Cases where the defendant represents itself as a member of the plaintiff association, as having a particular status or qualification, or even as being one and the same as the plaintiff association itself, are to be distinguished from ones in which the defendant passes its products off as having a specific quality characteristic of the products of the members of a particular association. In the

---

[10] (Scott V.-C., March 6, 1996).

[11] Council Regulation 1576/89. An application to strike out the statement of claim on the ground that the Regulation did not create private causes of action, failed.

[12] [1995] R.P.C. 16 (Aldous J.).

[13] (1931) 48 R.P.C. 565. The reasoning of *BMA v. Marsh* on this point has never carried conviction. In *Scotch Whisky Association v. J. D. Vinters, supra*, Scott V.-C. described the same argument in a related context as "a fanciful and unacceptable basis" for allowing the Association to sue for a breach of Community law.

[14] [1996] F.S.R. 739 (Rimer J.).

[15] As in *British Association of Aesthetic Plastic Surgeons v. Cambright* [1987] R.P.C. 549, the defendants were, in a colloquial sense, passing themselves off as something they were not; but were they passing themselves off as the plaintiffs?

former case, the association is the proper plaintiff in its own right because it directly suffers damage. In the latter, the association has, at best, *locus standi* to bring a representative action on behalf of its members,[16] who are the real victims of the passing-off.

Charities

It is now clear that a passing-off action lies at the suit of one charity even **2.17** against another bona fide charity, and *a fortiori* against a non-charitable defendant holding itself out as the plaintiff charity.[17] In *British Diabetic Association v. The Diabetic Society*[18] Walker J. followed the Australian, American and South African cases cited in the main work and held that the tort of passing-off was wide enough for the plaintiff charity to be granted relief against the three defendants, a small break-away charity with similar objectives and its two founders. On the facts, the plaintiffs failed to make out that they had a *de facto* exclusive reputation in the name The (British) Diabetic Society but the defendants' name was confusingly similar to the plaintiffs' official name and a final injunction was granted.

The jurisdiction of the court under the law of passing-off was not displaced by the concurrent statutory jurisdiction of the Charity Commissioners under section 6 of the Charities Act 1993 to order a registered charity to change its name if confusingly similar to that of another.

Churches

The Australian (*Church of the East*) and South African (*Old Apostolic*) cases **2.21** cited in the main work were approved by Walker J. in *British Diabetic Association v. The Diabetic Society.*[19]

Clubs

The position of a private members' club arose obliquely in *Harrods v.* **2.22** *Harrodian School*[20] with the implication that such a club could be a plaintiff in a passing-off action. The defendants' school was on the site of the former *Harrodian Club* but the club probably had little goodwill *vis-à-vis* the public at large since most of its members were Harrods employees, and any goodwill it may have had in its own right must have been abandoned when the club closed. Millett L.J. observed:

---

[16] Though *Consorzio Del Prosciutto Di Parma v. Marks & Spencer* [1991] R.P.C. 351 (C.A.) which was not cited by Scott V.-C. in the *Scotch Whisky* case, denies that a representative action can be brought by the association in such circumstances.

[17] The principle was also stated, obiter, in *Harrods v. Harrodian School*. See *infra* in relation to clubs.

[18] [1996] F.S.R. 1 (Robert Walker J.).

[19] [1996] F.S.R. 1 (Robert Walker J.).

[20] Court of Appeal, to be reported.

"The Plaintiffs rightly point out that the operation of a club for the benefit of employees is a trading activity, and that it would not matter if it were not; non-trading organisations such as clubs and charities are as much entitled to protection from passing-off as any one else. The Plaintiffs also submit that the Judge was wrong to disregard the separate but material reputation which the club acquired in Barnes as the staff club of Harrods.

In my view these criticisms are misplaced. The Judge was not distinguishing between trading and non-trading activities but between the use of the name 'Harrods' in relation to goods or services supplied to customers, that is to say in the course of a trading activity calculated to generate goodwill, and the use of the name 'Harrodian' in connection with a club provided as a facility for employees. The use of the club's name when hiring out its premises to members of the public was a minor and incidental extension of the latter usage. But in any case the Plaintiffs have neither pleaded nor established a reputation for running a club, and if the club acquired any goodwill of its own in the name *Harrodian* it was abandoned when the business of the club was discontinued."

C. CREATION OF GOODWILL

Trade preceded by advertising

2.27   The distinction drawn in the main work between reliance on pre-trading activities to generate goodwill as such, and their relevance to the existence of a misrepresentation by the defendant is well illustrated by *Law Society v. Griffiths*.[21] The plaintiffs were awarded an interlocutory injunction to protect the freephone number of their "Accident Line" service although the use by the defendants of a confusingly similar number narrowly anticipated the date of actual commencement of the plaintiffs' service. The plaintiffs' service and number had been promoted to solicitors and were about to be launched to the public on June 30, but there had been no more than "some seepage of information" about the scheme to the general public prior to that date. The defendants' number was selected on June 1, and was in use at least as early as June 27, although no publicity was planned for it until September. The defendants' principal submission that there was no misrepresentation to restrain failed on the facts, the time factor notwithstanding. That being the case, their submission that the Law Society could have no goodwill to protect until after June 30, was summarily dismissed as misconceived: the Society had ample goodwill in a variety of connected activities over a number of years and that goodwill would be damaged by the defendants' misrepresentation.

The proposition that pre-launch publicity can support a passing-off action was also approved in principle by Blackburne J. in *Labyrinth Media v. Brave*

---

[21] [1995] R.P.C. 16 (Aldous J.).

World[22] although on the facts the publicity relied on fell far short of the necessary standard. The plaintiffs and defendants both intended to launch videos of real life police car chases under the title *Police America* with the plaintiffs' video being second on the market. The plaintiffs obtained an *ex parte* injunction on the strength of a certain amount of pre-launch publicity but it was discharged at the *inter partes* hearing. Blackburne J. was prepared to say that he could see "no good reason why in an appropriate case a plaintiff may not establish his reputation in a product in advance of its release to the public simply by pre-launch publicity sufficient to enable it to mount a claim in passing-off." The decision of the Court of Appeal in *Marcus Publishing v. Hutton-Wild Communications*[23] did not preclude this and there were passages in all three judgments consistent with the possibility. However the only pre-launch publicity to have come to the attention of the general public was a single inconspicuous paragraph in *The Sun*, and although publicity to the trade had been more extensive there was no possibility of traders being deceived.

Glaxo v. Glaxowellcome[24] is worth mentioning briefly in this context for its affinities in reasoning with the Australian *General Motors* and *Fletcher Challenge* cases.

D. TERRITORIAL SCOPE OF GOODWILL

Borderline cases: to infer goodwill or not?

In *Jian Tools for Sales v. Roderick Manhattan Group*[25] Knox J., after an **2.36** extensive review of the authorities, held that the American plaintiffs had sufficient English goodwill in relation to their business plan software to obtain an interlocutory injunction. 127 sales, including review copies, were not *de minimis* and sales in England generated by foreign sources such as advertisements in American computer magazines should not be ignored. *Budweiser* was distinguished as a case where the plaintiffs' sales to PX customers and the American embassy were in a watertight compartment compared to the public at large, who could not buy the plaintiffs' beer however hard they tried. This is another case where the defendant had been in abortive negotiations to represent the plaintiff and suffered as a result, especially on the balance of convenience. They took a calculated risk with their eyes open.

In *Nice and Safe Attitude v. Flook*[26] such presence as the American National Space and Aeronautics Administration (NASA) had in England by virtue of scientific collaboration projects was too remote from the field of young persons' fashion for a licence by them to be effective as a defence against a company with actual goodwill in relation to *NASA* for clothing.

---

[22] [1995] EMLR 38 (Blackburne J.).
[23] [1990] R.P.C. 576, C.A.
[24] [1996] F.S.R. 388 (Lightman J.).
[25] [1995] F.S.R. 924 (Knox J.).
[26] (Robert Walker J., February 8, 1996).

E. FOREIGN PLAINTIFFS: AN INTERNATIONAL OVERVIEW

Australia

2.43 The publishers of an internationally-known Arabic language newspaper, *Al Hayat*, were granted an interlocutory injunction although it was not distributed in Australia: *Al Hayat Publishing v. Sokarno*.[27] The defendant had taken part in abortive negotiations to publish the paper in Australia, and had applied to register *Al Hayat* in his own name, so there was a clear implicit concession that the name was valuable.

Canada

2.46 Although the plaintiffs in *Walt Disney v. Triple Five*[28] obtained an injunction against an indoor theme park at a Canadian shopping mall operating as *Fantasyland*, in *Walt Disney v. Fantasyland Hotel*[29] they failed in respect of the same name for an Hotel at the same shopping mall. The Alberta Court of Appeal held that liability of the hotel was not *res judicata* as a result of the successful action against the theme park, and that passing-off was not made out. In terms which are rather closer to English law than the previous decision, the court held:

> "The appellant says [that] the respondent in using the name Fantasyland for its hotel, is creating the false impression that it is authorized or connected with the appellant, in other words, the respondent is, 'cashing in' on the appellant's goodwill.
>
> The appellant's theory of the law of passing-off contains a fatal weakness. Even the 'more common type of passing-off' referred to requires proof of the essentials of goodwill; misrepresentation or confusion, which the trial judge found, as a fact, did not exist in this case. In other words, the allegation or even the belief that the respondent is benefiting from the use of the name Fantasyland is not enough to found the tort of passing-off. The British Columbia cases cited do not support a modification in the requirements for the tort of passing-off."

In *Enterprise Rent-A-Car Co. v. Singer*[30] an American car hire company were the first to have goodwill in relation to the name Enterprise in Canada and obtained an injunction at trial against a Canadian company using the same name. Canadians had used its services on visits to the United States and it had conducted some leasing transactions in Canada. One reason from dismissing the Canadian company's cross-action was that they came to the Court with

---

[27] (1996) 34 I.P.R. 214 (Tamberlin J., Federal Court).
[28] (1994) 53 C.P.R. (3d) 129, noted in the main work.
[29] (1996) 67 C.P.R. (3d) 444 (Court of Appeal, Alberta).
[30] (1996) 66 C.P.R. (3d) 543 (Federal Court, McKeown, J.).

unclean hands, having adopted the name knowing of the plaintiffs and their plans to expand.[31] The defendants' use was also too small-scale and too late, since the plaintiffs had begun to generate Canadian goodwill by the time it started.

India

Further Indian cases adopting the "soft" line of authority are *William Grant*   **2.48**
v. McDowell[32] and *Calvin Klein v. International Apparel Syndicate,*[33] although both were probably strong enough on the facts to have been decided the same way in England.

H. DEALINGS WITH GOODWILL

Assignment of business premises

Examples

In *Harrods v. Harrodian School*[34] the defendants adopted the name *Harrodian*   **2.73**
from the *Harrodian Club* (a sports and social club for the plaintiffs' employees) formerly on the premises which they had purchased from the plaintiffs. It could not be said that this entitled them to use the name or gave them any immunity from suit, but it was relevant to rebut a charge that the defendants' proprietor had chosen the name with intent to deceive.[35] The plaintiffs had even left a large signboard for *The Harrodian Club* in their house script and colours on the site, but the defendants would have probably been liable to an injunction to remove it, had they not done so before trial.

I. SHARED OR QUALIFIED OWNERSHIP OF GOODWILL

Corporate groups, house marks

In *William Grant v. Glen Catrine Bonded Warehouse*[36] the second and third   **2.83**
pursuers were held by the Court of Session to have *locus standi* to sue although the relevant goodwill of the former *Grant's* company had been assigned to its holding company (the first pursuers) to be held "for its own use

---

[31] Following *Brewster Transport v. Rocky Mountain Tours* [1931] 1 D.L.R. 713 (S. Ct. of Canada) cited in the main work.

[32] [1994] F.S.R. 690 (Mahinder Narain J., Delhi).

[33] [1995] F.S.R. 515 (Mrs Justice Ruma Pal, Calcutta).

[34] Court of Appeal, to be reported.

[35] Sir Michael Kerr, dissenting, pointedly observed that the name of the site would have been markedly less attractive if it had formerly been owned by *Woolworths* or a Borstal.

[36] [1995] S.L.T. 936 (Lord Abernethy, Outer House).

and for the use of . . . its subsidiary companies." This was not an assignment in gross so as to disentitle any of the pursuers to sue.

> "In *Pinto v. Badman* the assignment of a trade mark became completely separated from the business with which it was associated. It came into the hands of a third party. In *Thorneloe v. Hill* the same thing happened with a trade name. In that situation it is easy to see why the assignment was held to be of no effect. As Fry L.J. put it in *Pinto v. Badman* (at (1891) 8 R.P.C. 194–195): 'It [the trade mark] cannot be assigned when it is divorced from its place of origin, or when, in the hands of the transferee, it would indicate something different to what it indicated in the hands of the transferor.'

> That, in my opinion, is the rationale behind the rule. If the trade mark or trade name is truly separated from the business to which it was attached, then its use is, as Romer J. put it in *Thorneloe v. Hill* (at p. 577), a fraud on the public. But that is not at all what has happened in this case. The goodwill attaching to the name 'Grant's' has not been truly separated from the underlying business. Continued use of the name does not in any way indicate something different from what it indicated prior to the transfer. Its continued use is in no sense a fraud on the public. In my opinion, in a situation such as exists in this case, the goodwill attaching to the name 'Grant's' is goodwill which belongs to every part of the group business and how that group business is organised within the group is irrelevant for present purposes."

Multinationals and parallel imports

2.84 *Revlon v. Cripps & Lee*[37] was followed in Canada in *Smith & Nephew v. Glen Oak*.[38] An interlocutory injunction granted in favour of the licensee of the German proprietor of the *Nivea* trade mark in respect of parallel imports of *Nivea* from Mexico was discharged on appeal. The plaintiff, as licensee, had no independent goodwill to protect and could not assert such rights as it had against goods directly or indirectly originating from its licensor.

J. EXTINCTION AND REVIVAL OF GOODWILL

Abandoned goodwill cannot be revived

2.90 In *Harrods v. Harrodian School*,[39] any goodwill attaching to the plaintiffs' former Harrodian Club had been abandoned when the club closed in 1990,

---

[37] [1980] F.S.R. 85 (C.A.).
[38] (1996) 68 C.P.R. (3d) 153 (Federal Court of Appeal).
[39] Court of Appeal, to be reported.

three years before the defendants' school was launched. Other goods or services for which the plaintiffs had used the word *Harrodian* as well as some education-related services provided under the *Harrods* name, had been discontinued long before.

DAMAGE

A. THE IMPORTANCE OF DAMAGE IN THE PAST AND TODAY

Damage as the "acid test" for passing-off

3.03 The conflicting views on the importance and nature of damage in the modern law of passing-off are well illustrated by the judgments of the Court of Appeal in *Harrods v. Harrodian School*[1] Harman J. dismissed the action at trial, holding that there was no likelihood of confusion, but did not deal separately with the issue of damage. The majority (Millett and Beldam L.JJ.) affirmed in terms consistent with the treatment of damage in *Stringfellow v. McCain.*[2] In a dissenting judgment, Sir Michael Kerr would have allowed the plaintiffs' appeal. He would have held that:

---

[1] Court of Appeal, to be reported.
[2] [1984] R.P.C. 501; [1984] F.S.R. 199, C.A.

12

"Loss of distinctiveness causes damage to a reputation for excellence, and loss of trade will ultimately follow. The authorities show two relevant propositions in this regard. First, a debasement or dilution of the plaintiffs reputation, as the result of the action of the defendant, is a relevant head of damage. Secondly, if the act which constitutes the passing-off has the effect of raising in people's minds the mistaken belief of a connection between the defendant and the plaintiff, but which is in fact non-existent, then the court will have regard to the fact that the plaintiff has, to that extent, lost control of his reputation, and that he has therefore suffered damage to his goodwill by a potentially injurious association with the defendant against which the court will protect him by injunction."

From the words "potentially injurious association" as well as other passages it is clear that to Sir Michael Kerr, the mere loss of exclusivity or control of the name *Harrods* was damage enough: it was irrelevant that the defendants might not be taken as having any connection at all with the plaintiffs, or that there was nothing currently or foreseeably disreputable or discreditable about their business. Citing but distinguishing *Taittinger v. Allbev*[3] where (to quote Bingham M.R. the defendants' conduct would "debase or cheapen" the plaintiffs' reputation he went on:

"In fairness to the defendants, it cannot of course be said in the present case that a similar consequence would necessarily follow, and indeed it is greatly to be hoped that this would not be the case. But that is not the test. The crucial point, as stated in the second of the foregoing propositions, is the plaintiff's inevitable loss of control of his reputation and the consequent risk of damage to it."

As a third head of damage Sir Michael alluded to the argument that the plaintiffs would have to abandon their proposed use of *Harrodian* in relation to various facilities at the *Harrods House Hotel* which they planned to open.[4]

The problem with a strong dissenting judgment is that it gives expression to the very arguments which have been rejected by the majority. If any of the heads of damage identified in the main text as "reputation in defendant's hands"; "restriction on expansion"; "loss of exclusivity" or "dilution" were sufficient to support a passing-off action in their own right, then Harrods should have won. That they did not, shows that damage is still an independent and essential element of the tort alongside misrepresentation and goodwill. Millett L.J. in the majority noted the inconsistency of relying on one specific

---

[3] [1993] F.S.R. 641 (C.A.).

[4] This seems excessively pessimistic. They would hardly be liable for passing-off at the suit of the defendants, and if the name *Harrodian* was marginally less desirable as a result of its use by the school that hardly turned it into a liability. Total exclusivity is not a necessary pre-requisite for the name of a bar, health club or cookery school.

head of damage, erosion of distinctiveness, which arose independently of one of the other essential elements of the tort:

> "I have an intellectual difficulty in accepting the concept that the law insists upon the presence of both confusion and damage and yet recognises as sufficient a head of damage which does not depend on confusion."

The same applies to the other heads relied on by Sir Michael Kerr: they can arise independently of any misrepresentation, the interest protected is not the plaintiff's goodwill, and they debase the element of damage to a mere circularity, a legal fiction.

B. THE REQUIREMENT TO PROVE DAMAGE IN PRACTICE

A rule of reason

3.11 Beldam L.J. in *Harrods v. Harrodian School*[5] explained the interrelation between the extent of confusion, and the likelihood that confusion would be damaging. On the facts, and given the very distinct fields of activity of the parties, the plaintiffs had failed to prove their case.

> "The risk of significant damage to the appellant's goodwill and reputation from the activities of the defendant depends not only on the nature and strength of the connection made by the public who perceive a link in the name notwithstanding the different spheres of activity, but also on how many of those persons would in consequence regard shortcomings in the running of the school as reflecting adversely on the quality of the goods and services offered in the department store and on its reputation as a supplier of such goods and services and so whether any customer or potential customer is likely to withhold, withdraw or reduce his custom or consider the appellant's reputation for excellence to be diminished."

C. HEADS OF DAMAGE

Reputation in defendant's hands

3.21 See para. 3.03 *supra*.

---

[5] Court of Appeal, to be reported.

Restriction on expansion

See para. 3.03 *supra*. **3.22**

Loss of exclusivity; erosion or swamping of distinctiveness

See paras. 3.03 *supra* and 3.24 *infra*. **3.23**

Dilution: damage without confusion

A relatively narrow interpretation of the *Elderflower Champagne* case[6] was **3.24** given by the Court of Appeal in *Harrods v. Harrodian School*[7] where Millett L.J., for the majority, rejected an argument that *Harrods* department store would suffer a similar kind of damage from the existence of the *Harrodian School*, even in the absence of confusion between the plaintiffs' store and the defendants' school.[8]

> "In *Taittinger SA v. Allbev Ltd* the court appears to have recognised a different head of damage.[9] If the defendants were allowed to market their product under the name Elderflower Champagne:
>
>> 'there would take place a blurring or erosion of the uniqueness that now attends the word "champagne", so that the exclusive reputation of the champagne houses would be debased' (per Peter Gibson L.J. at p. 669 of the [FSR] report).
>
> It is self-evident that the application of the plaintiff's brand name to inferior goods is likely to injure the plaintiffs' reputation and damage his goodwill if people take the inferior goods to be those of the plaintiff. That is a classic head of damage in cases of passing-off. But Peter Gibson L.J. may have had more in mind than this. He referred without disapproval to the submission of Counsel for the plaintiffs that if the defendants were allowed to continue to call their product Elderflower Champagne:
>
>> 'the effect would be to demolish the distinctiveness of the word champagne, and that would inevitably damage the goodwill of the champagne houses.'
>
> Erosion of the distinctiveness of a brand name has been recognised as a form of damage to the goodwill of the business with which the name is connected in a number of cases, particularly in Australia and New Zealand; but unless care is taken this could mark an unacceptable extension to the tort of passing off. To date the law has not sought to

---

[6] [1993] F.S.R. 641, C.A.
[7] Court of Appeal, to be reported.
[8] Sir Michael Kerr dissented, see above.
[9] As compared to *Lego v. Lego M. Lemelstrich*, treated here as a case where there was a real risk of the defendant's goods, though non-competitive, being taken for those of the plaintiffs.

protect the value of the brand name as such, but the value of the goodwill which it generates; and it insists on proof of confusion to justify its intervention. But the erosion of the distinctiveness of a brand name which occurs by reason of its degeneration into common use as a generic term is not necessarily dependent on confusion at all. The danger that if the defendant's product was called champagne then all sparkling wines would eventually come to be called champagne would still exist even if no one was deceived into thinking that such wine really was champagne. I have an intellectual difficulty in accepting the concept that the law insists upon the presence of both confusion and damage and yet recognises as sufficient a head of damage which does not depend on confusion. Counsel for the Plaintiffs relied strongly on the possibility of damage of this nature, but it is in my opinion not necessary to consider it further in the present case. There is no danger of 'Harrods' becoming a generic term for a retail emporium in the luxury class, and if such a danger existed the use of a different name in connection with an institution of a different kind would not advance the process."[10]

It is implicit in this treatment of *Taittinger v. Allbev* that the result depended on the very close proximity of the fields of business of the parties. Self-evidently, *Champagne* is severely at risk of losing its distinctiveness and suffering a descent to merely generic status if the term is used for sparkling wines in general, and the same risk exists to some extent if it is used for other sparkling beverages, even fruit-flavoured water. However, use of *Champagne* for wholly unrelated goods, such as perfume or soap, cannot possibly affect the question of whether *Champagne* is at risk of becoming generic in relation to sparkling drinks; any more than the distinctive quality of *Scotch* for whisky is at risk because Scotch eggs and *Scotch* brand adhesive tape do not come from Scotland. In reality, this head of damage in *Taittinger v. Allbev* was not dilution in the American sense at all, but simply an aspect of the familiar one of loss of distinctive character considered at para. 2.23 of the main work.

---

[10] Is it unfair to suggest that Sir Michael Kerr, who was so concerned to protect the name of *Harrods* against erosion of its distinctiveness, should have hesitated before saying that "*Rolls Royce* ... has come to be used colloquially as an adjective to express the highest possible standard."? Be that as it may, *Rolls Royce* has not become generic for luxury motor cars, aero-engines or anything else.

CHAPTER 4

MISREPRESENTATION: GENERAL PRINCIPLES

17

A. THE ESSENTIAL MISREPRESENTATION

No monopoly in name, mark or get-up

4.02 *Harrods v. Harrodian School*[1] affirms that there is no monopoly in a name as such, even one as well-known and distinctive as *Harrods*. Liability depends on whether in all the circumstances the defendants' use is calculated to deceive. That is why the success of the defendants on the facts of that case does not imply that they would be have been allowed to call their school *Harrods School* or use the plaintiffs' distinctive script or livery. A sufficiently explicit or outrageous representation of a connection with Harrods would have overcome the effect of the parties' very different fields of activity. Conversely, it did not follow that an "enterprising trader" would have been allowed to set up a retail shop under the name *The Harrodian*.

> "It is well settled that (unless registered as a trade mark) no one has a monopoly in his brand name or get up, however familiar these may be. Passing off is a wrongful invasion of a right of property vested in the plaintiff; but the property which is protected by an action for passing off is not the plaintiff's proprietary right in the name or get up which the defendant has misappropriated but the goodwill and reputation of his business which is likely to be harmed by the defendant's misrepresentation.[2]
>
> It is this fundamental principle of the law of passing off which leads me to reject the main way in which the Plaintiffs have put their case before us. [. . .] The name 'Harrods' may be universally recognised, but the business with which it is associated in the minds of the public is not all-embracing. To be known to everyone is not to be known for everything."

Examples of actionable misrepresentations

4.03 Recognition of wider categories of misrepresentation is making some progress. In *SDS Biotech v. Power*[3] both parties marketed a fungicide with a MAFF number denoting it had been approved for use by the Government. In the case of the defendants, such approval had not been given and they were not entitled to use the MAFF number. Applications by the plaintiffs for Order 14 judgment, and by the defendants to strike out the statement of claim were both refused. Difficult points of law arose which were inappropriate to determine on motion.

---

[1] Court of Appeal, to be reported.
[2] Citations omitted.
[3] (1989) [1995] F.S.R. 797 (Aldous J.).

SDS Biotech v. Power was considered in *Hodge Clemco v. Airblast*[4] where the defendants sold replacement lenses as "to suit" or as "suitable for" for the plaintiffs' sand-blasting helmets. The replacements were safe, but their use would be illegal because they did not have the necessary approval under the COSHH Regulations. Jacob J. held that it was at least arguable that stating that the defendants' lenses were "to suit" the plaintiffs' helmets, or simply selling them for that purpose, amounted to an implicit misrepresentation that their use would be legal for that purpose and that although the plaintiffs' standing to complain about such a misrepresentation as passing-off was arguable either way, the necessary standard for an interlocutory injunction had been met. However, the balance of convenience favoured the defendants and an injunction was refused.

B. THE MATERIALITY OF THE MISREPRESENTATION

Misrepresentations not operative at time of purchase

BASF v. CEP[5] is another example of a case where, if there was any **4.08** misrepresentation at all, it was so transient as to be immaterial. A glance at the cover of the defendants' *Farming Opus* directory might suggest a connection with the plaintiffs' *Opus* pesticide, but the mistake could not survive reading inside.

Relationship of the misrepresentation to *locus standi* to sue

See para. 4.03 discussing *SDS Biotech v. Power*[6] and *Hodge Clemco v.* **4.09** *Airblast*.[7]

C. USE OF NAME OR MARK WITHOUT MISREPRESENTATION

Accessories, consumables, spare parts etc

In *Hodge Clemco v. Airblast*[8] there was arguably passing-off by selling **4.11** accessories for the plaintiffs' sand-blasting helmets whose use would be illegal. See para. 4.03.

---

[4] [1995] F.S.R. 806 (Jacob J.).
[5] (Knox J., October 26, 1995).
[6] (1989) [1995] F.S.R. 797 (Aldous J.).
[7] [1995] F.S.R. 806 (Jacob J.).
[8] [1995] F.S.R. 806 (Jacob J.).

D. THE DEFENDANT NEED NOT ACT FRAUDULENTLY

Fraud and instruments of deception

4.21 The defendants in *Modus Vivendi (Ronson) v. Keen*[9] were fraudulent, and their liability for exporting instruments of deception cannot have been based on joint tortfeasorship since the actual passing off took place in China and Chinese law was not relied on. The get-up of the goods was clearly calculated, in both senses, to deceive.

E. EFFECT OF FRAUD WHERE SHOWN

Evidential value of fraud

4.23 The evidential value of fraud was acknowledged in *Harrods v. Harrodian School*[10] but the plaintiffs failed in a concerted attack on the bona fides of the defendants' proprietor. The trial judge found that his intention was not to deceive the public or to exploit the name and reputation of Harrods, but to take legitimate advantage of the name of the site of the former *Harrodian Club* as such. Collateral attacks on his conduct in negotiations which eventually led to the purchase of the site of the *Harrodian Club*; and in enforcing an order for costs against the plaintiffs by writ of *fi. fa.* after trial also failed. In the latter case, the implication that he entertained a certain amount of resentment against the plaintiffs in 1995, after undergoing a bruising trial in 1994, was useless to prove that in 1993 he had intended to trade off Harrods' reputation.

F. THE DEFENDANT NEED NOT COMPETE WITH THE PLAINTIFF

Shelf and dormant companies as defendants

4.28/A Two cases demonstrate different approaches to the problem of companies being registered under a particular name, not with any intention of trading but perhaps simply in the hope of being bought out for an inflated amount by a business with a genuine commercial interest in the name. In *Glaxo v. Glaxowellcome*[11] there was widespread publicity for the forthcoming merger of the Glaxo and Wellcome companies with the intended name Glaxo-Wellcome plc. The individual defendants, a company registration agent and his mother, registered a company under the name Glaxowellcome Ltd and

---

[9] (Lightman J., July 5, 1995).
[10] Court of Appeal, to be reported.
[11] [1996] F.S.R. 388 (Lightman J.).

demanded (in purportedly "without prejudice" correspondence) £100,000 from the plaintiffs to sell it. Lightman J. described the defendants' conduct as "A dishonest scheme to appropriate the goodwill of the two plaintiffs and to extort from the plaintiffs a substantial sum as the price for not damaging the plaintiffs' goodwill in the names Glaxo and Wellcome." He granted interlocutory mandatory injunctions to change the company's name, but although his judgment dwells at length on the individual defendants' manifest bad faith it does not explain, other than by analogy with some unspecified cases, how this "pre-emptive strike" by the defendants amounted to passing-off[12] or any other cause of action known to the common law.

In *Ben & Jerrys Homemade Inc. v. Ben & Jerrys Ice Cream Ltd*[13] the American plaintiffs, an ice-cream company, found on attempting to establish a subsidiary in the United Kingdom that there was already a shelf company on the Register with a similar name. In contrast to the *Glaxowellcome* case the defendants did not attempt to extort any money and the plaintiffs did not seek a mandatory injunction for a change of name but only a *quia timet* interlocutory injunction against the defendant company commencing to trade in the ice-cream market under its registered name. Since the proprietors of the company expressly had no such intention, and there was delay, Ferris J. refused the injunction.

Dealing with the broader situation, two fundamental difficulties always arise. The first is that the mere existence of a company on the Register under a particular name can hardly be regarded as a misrepresentation in its own right, even if it does not go wholly unnoticed. If it were otherwise, then any passing-off case between two English companies with similar names would be open and shut in favour of the plaintiff, even if, for instance, they traded in such disparate fields that no confusion was possible in reality.[14] Even if this difficulty can be overcome, the second problem is that passing-off is about misrepresentations made by a trader in the course of trade. A shelf company which does not trade at all can hardly be liable for passing-off. At most, its unexplained existence is an equivocal threat of passing-off to come. *Glaxo-wellcome* goes halfway to avoiding this difficulty, since one of the individual defendants was a company registration agent who was self-evidently sued in his trading capacity. There is a third difficulty which will sometimes arise but is not inevitable. Since the object of the defendant is to forestall the plaintiff in its choice of name, it may happen that the plaintiff will have no goodwill in the jurisdiction; either because one is dealing with an overseas plaintiff expanding as in *Ben & Jerrys* or with a totally new venture. This was not a

---

[12] If that is what Lightman J. intended. It is possible that he only relied on the passing-off cases to show that an interlocutory mandatory injunction to change one's name was not unprecedented.

[13] (1995) 33 I.P.R. 157 (Ferris J.).

[14] Some cases in the late nineteenth or early twentieth century seem to ignore this, but that was before the law of passing-off took its present form and the outcome may have depended on the Companies Acts then in force, which gave greater statutory protection against companies with similar names co-existing on the Register. It would also have been taken for granted that the defendant company would trade in due course, and its intended field of business would have been defined with some precision in the Memorandum of Incorporation.

problem in *Glaxowellcome* because the existing Glaxo and Wellcome companies (rather than a newly formed merged body, as in the Australian *Fletcher Challenge* case) were plaintiffs. Finally, the non-availability of a preferred name is, at best, a very weak head of damage to rely on and it is hard to see what other damage the plaintiff suffers. Whether passing-off has three essential elements or five, more than half of them seem to be missing.

Before condemning the practical consequences of a strict application of the law, two points need to be borne in mind. The first is that a company which merely exists on the Register without trading acquires no rights, so far as the law of passing-off is concerned, to prevent another company using even precisely the same name in any line of business.[15] Passing-off protects a trader's goodwill, and a shelf company which has never traded can by definition have no goodwill. Its rights, such as they are, are confined to blocking the registration of another company with an identical name.[16] The second point is that even if the shelf company were to begin to trade under its registered name, its prior registration would not confer any immunity from suit. A defence of antecedent user would require actual use of the name in trade, so as to generate goodwill. If the defence of use of one's own name exists at all for a company, it is defeated by *mala fides*. A defence of acquiescence would obviously not arise until the plaintiff had an opportunity to sue, and in any event would be excluded by putting the defendant on notice.

Common field of activity unnecessary . . .

4.29   The celebrated dictum of Wynn-Parry J. in *McCulloch v. May*[17] has now been repudiated by the Court of Appeal in *Harrods v. Harrodian School*[18] as discredited and contrary to authority: "There is no requirement that the defendant should be carrying on a business which competes with that of the plaintiff or which would compete with any natural extension of the plaintiff's business." The absence of a common field of activity between the plaintiffs' department store and the defendants' preparatory school was therefore not fatal as a matter of law, but was highly relevant to the conclusion that there was no risk of confusion. As in *Stringfellow v. McCain*,[19] the burden of proving confusion and damage was a heavy one when there was no overlap, or only a tenuous overlap, in the parties' respective fields of activity. Customers of Harrods would be incredulous if they were told that Harrods had opened a preparatory school:

---

[15] Compare *Maxim's v. Dye* [1977] F.S.R. 364, where it was completely irrelevant that the owners of *Maxim's* restaurant in Paris were a company registered in England. They succeeded because they had English goodwill, not because of an English corporate registration.

[16] Suppose Wellcome had registered *Glaxowellcome* to strengthen its defence to Glaxo's bid: would this have been regarded as anything more than a futile and even childish distraction?

[17] [1947] 2 All E.R. 845; 65 R.P.C. 58 (Wynn-Parry J.).

[18] Court of Appeal, to be reported.

[19] [1984] R.P.C. 501; [1984] F.S.R. 199, C.A.

"The question is whether there is a real risk that members of the public will be deceived into thinking that a school called *The Harrodian School* (not written in the distinctive Harrods script or livery) is owned or managed by Harrods or under Harrods' supervision or control."

Illustrations of degree

In *BASF v. CEP*[20] the plaintiffs' use of *Opus* for pesticides did not entitle them **4.31** to an injunction against *Farming Opus* for a trade directory. It was obviously not a BASF publication.

G. TO WHOM MAY THE MISREPRESENTATION BE MADE?

Prospective customers and ultimate consumers

The main work notes the anomaly in Lord Diplock's formulation of passing-off in *Advocaat*, where he speaks of the misrepresentation being made to customers of the defendant. In *Harrods v. Harrodian School*[21] the trial judge was criticised for supposedly looking for evidence of confusion only among those members of the public who had enquired about sending their children to the defendants' school. The Court of Appeal (Millet and Beldam L.JJ., Sir Michael Kerr dissenting) rejected the criticism on the facts, and put the question in terms of whether there would be "confusion among the common customers of the parties,"—the broad section of the public for whom both parties catered in their different fields of business: **4.33**

"In the course of argument before us the Judge was criticised for having considered only those members of the public who had made enquiry of the school with a view to sending their children there. It was submitted that he wrongly allowed himself to be influenced by the consideration that the choice of a fee-paying school for one's children is not an impulse purchase, and that a parent who was considering the Defendants' school for his children would be likely to make sufficient enquiries to eliminate any potential confusion that might otherwise occur. This would have been wrong, for the relevant public is not confined to parents who take up places at the school. The Plaintiffs and the Defendants appeal to a common section of the public—affluent members of the middle class who live in London, shop at Harrods and wish to send their children to fee-paying schools. They are the persons who must be kept in mind when considering the likelihood of confusion."

---

[20] (Knox J., October 26, 1995).
[21] Court of Appeal, to be reported.

Customer who do not have to pay for goods

4.34   For passing-off by choice of a freephone telephone number see *Law Society v. Griffiths.*[22] In *Jian Tools for Sales v. Roderick Manhattan Group*[23] Knox J. refused to disregard instances in which the plaintiffs' software had been given away free for review, since though these could not be described as sales to consumers, they were relevant to whether the plaintiffs had goodwill in the jurisdiction.

Miscellaneous cases

4.36   In *Law Society v. Griffiths*[24] the relevant misrepresentees were victims of accidents or injuries who wished to contact the plaintiffs' referral scheme which had the telephone number 0500 192939. The defendant firm of solicitors were restrained from using the number 0800 192939. Both numbers were free to callers, and in the case of the Law Society the result of a call was that the caller was referred to a member of the Society's personal injury panel.

I. WHO IS LIABLE FOR PASSING-OFF?

Individual defendants; directors, officers and proprietors

4.43   In *Glaxo v. Glaxowellcome*[25] Lightman J. granted interlocutory mandatory injunctions requiring the promoters of the defendant company to change its name, but the reasoning is not entirely satisfactory.

J. INSTRUMENTS OF DECEPTION

Exports of deceptive goods

4.49   The applicability of the doctrine of instruments of deception to goods exported from the United Kingdom can have effects which are perhaps surprising if the nature of the jurisdiction is not kept in sight; as the practical effect of such relief may be not far short of an extra-territorial or even World-wide injunction. In *Modus Vivendi (Ronson) v. Keen*[26] the plaintiffs' claim for damages (an injunction was not sought for extraneous reasons) arose from

---

[22] [1995] R.P.C. 16 (Aldous J.).
[23] [1995] F.S.R. 924 (Knox J.).
[24] [1995] R.P.C. 16 (Aldous J.).
[25] [1996] F.S.R. 388 (Lightman J.). See also *British Diabetic Association v. Diabetic Society* para. 2.17.
[26] (Lightman J., July 5, 1995).

passing-off in China, but as Lightman J. explained, England was the proper forum and English law applied[27]:

> "Ronson's case is that its cans in China had a distinctive get-up . . . and that Keen abandoned the distinctive get-up of the Newport can in favour of a get-up similar to the Ronson can, so as to lead and with the effect of leading customers familiar with Ronson's cans to buy Keen's in the belief that they were those of Ronson. It is perhaps somewhat surprising that a trial as to the existence of Ronson's goodwill in China and as to whether customers in China have been misled by Keen should be tried in England according to principles of English law, and that there has been no trial before a court in China or (at this trial) any references to the law of China. But this is because Keen's cans were manufactured in England and sold to Keen's exclusive distributor in Hong Kong for onward sale to and in China, and in these circumstances, if Ronson's allegations are true, since the 'instruments of deception' (Keen's cans) were put into circulation in this jurisdiction, under English law the tort of passing-off has been committed in England, though the damage, in respect of which compensation is sought in this action, has been suffered outside the jurisdiction i.e. in China. Accordingly, not only is England the proper forum for the trial, but English law is the proper law to apply in deciding whether Keen's conduct constitutes a tort giving rise to a claim in damages."

In Scotland, confirmation that liability for the export of deceptive goods arises under the law of the place from which the goods are exported is found in *William Grant v. Glen Catrine Bonded Warehouse*.[28] An argument by the defenders that liability arose, if at all, under the double actionability rule of *Phillips v. Eyre* failed. The pursuers did not have to plead or prove that the defenders' conduct would have been actionable in any of the numerous jurisdictions to which the defenders exported and where the pursuers claimed, in general terms, to have a goodwill to protect.

Liability for passing-off abroad

Actions in England for passing-off or unfair competition abroad are now governed by the provisions of the Private International Law (Miscellaneous Provisions) Act 1995.[29] The Act abolishes the former rule of "double actionability," otherwise known as the rule in *Phillips v. Eyre*, in favour of the   **4.50**

---

[27] Compare *Dixon & Son v. George Richardson* (1933) 50 R.P.C. 365 (Palatine Court), again concerned with the get-up of goods exported to China. The plaintiffs failed on the facts. Although the Chinese Trade Mark Bureau had already held that there was no possibility of confusion this was not conclusive (indeed, it was neither pleaded nor addressed in the judgment) and the issue of deceptive similarity was examined *do novo* on the evidence before the court.

[28] [1995] S.L.T. 936 (Lord Abernethy, Outer House).

[29] Part III of the Act was brought into force on May 1, 1996 by The Private International Law (Miscellaneous Provisions) Act 1995 Commencement Order 1996 (S.I. 1996 No. 995) which is subject to the transitional provisions of section 14 of the Act.

simple application in most cases of the law of the place where the tort occurred. However, the *lex loci delicti commissi* itself may be displaced in favour of the "proper law of the tort" (although that phrase is not used in the Act) if there are sufficiently important factors connecting the tort with another country. In the application of the Act to passing-off, the normal and perhaps invariable rule will be that the *lex loci delicti commissi* applies unmodified.

The principal sections of the Act relevant to passing-off and unfair competition actions are sections 9, 10, 11 and 12, set out below. Section 13 preserves double actionability for defamation claims and section 14 creates a general public policy exception.

Section 9: Purpose of Part III

(1) The rules in this Part apply for choosing the law (in this Part referred to as "the applicable law") to be used for determining issues relating to tort or (for the purposes of the law of Scotland) delict.

(2) The characterisation for the purposes of private international law of issues arising in a claim as issues relating to tort or delict is a matter for the courts of the forum.

(3) The rules in this Part do not apply in relation to issues arising in any claim excluded from the operation of this Part by section 13 below.[30]

(4) The applicable law shall be used for determining the issues arising in a claim, including in particular the question whether an actionable tort or delict has occurred.

(5) The applicable law to be used for determining the issues arising in a claim shall exclude any choice of law rules forming part of the law of the country or countries concerned.

[...]

Section 10. Abolition of certain common law rules

The rules of the common law, in so far as they—

(a) require actionability under both the law of the forum and the law of another country for the purpose of determining whether a tort or delict is actionable; or

(b) allow (as an exception from the rules falling within paragraph (a) above) for the law of a single country to be applied for the purpose of determining the issues, or any of the issues, arising in the case in question,

---

[30] Principally defamation claims.

are hereby abolished so far as they apply to any claim in tort or delict which is not excluded from the operation of this Part by section 13 below.

Section 11. Choice of applicable law: the general rule

(1) The general rule is that the applicable law is the law of the country in which the events constituting the tort or delict in question occur.

(2) Where elements of those events occur in different countries, the applicable law under the general rule is to be taken as being—

[. . .]³¹

(c) in any other case, the law of the country in which the most significant element or elements of those events occurred.

Section 12. Choice of applicable law: displacement of the general rule

(1) If it appears, in all circumstances, from a comparison of—

(a) the significance of the factors which connect a tort or delict with the country whose law would be the applicable law under the general rule; and

(b) the significance of any factors connecting the tort or delict with another country,

that it is substantially more appropriate for the applicable law for determining the issues arising in the case, or any of those issues, to be the law of the other country, the general rule is displaced and the applicable law for determining those issues or that issue (as the case may be) is the law of that other country.

(2) The factors that may be taken into account as connecting a tort or delict with a country for the purposes of this section include, in particular, factors relating to the parties, to any of the events which constitute the tort or delict in question or to any of the circumstances or consequences of those events.

In contrast to some other intellectual property torts, there has never been any difficulty in suing in England in respect of passing off abroad, provided that the double actionability requirement could be met. The practical effect of the Act in the context of passing-off is that in future actions in England for unfair competition abroad will continue to be possible, but the applicable law under the 1995 Act will almost certainly be the *lex loci delicti commissi*. English law, as the *lex fori*, will cease to have any relevance unless the act of unfair competition is characterised as analogous to injurious falsehood, in which case section 13 preserves double actionability.

---

³¹ Subsections omitted relate to personal injuries and damage to property.

K. THE TIME FACTOR

Start of conduct complained of

4.53 See also *Jian Tools for Sales v. Roderick Manhattan Group*[32] and the cases cited at para. 2.27.

---

[32] [1995] F.S.R. 924 (Knox J.).

ACTIONABLE MISREPRESENTATIONS

D. DECEPTION AS TO IDENTITY OR BUSINESS CONNECTION

The general principle

The applicability of the principle of *Ewing v. Buttercup Margarine*[1] depends **5.21** on whether, in all the circumstances, a connection will be assumed to exist in a form damaging to the plaintiffs. So in *Wagamama v. City Centre Restaurants*,[2] where both parties ran restaurants (though in different market sectors) damage was inherently likely, though in *Harrods v. Harrodian School*[3] the difference between a department store and a preparatory school meant that

---

[1] [1917] 2 Ch. 1; 34 R.P.C. 232, C.A.
[2] [1995] F.S.R. 713 (Laddie J.).
[3] Court of Appeal, to be reported.

confusion would be minimal, and unlikely to damage the plaintiffs to the limited extent it might occur.

In *Law Society v. Griffiths*[4] Aldous J. dealt with an argument that in adopting a freephone telephone number which differed from that of the plaintiffs only by one digit, the defendants were not making any misrepresentation:

> "Despite that evidence,[5] the defendants believe that the plaintiffs' complaint is really one of unfair trading and not passing off. The defendants are right that a misrepresentation must be established, but are wrong in believing that it requires an express statement. A person who adopts the mantle of another can by his silence misrepresent that he is that other. Thus a person who selects a confusingly similar telephone number or a similar name may well represent that he is that other by either saying so or by failing to take steps when telephoned or called to disabuse the person who is making the telephone call. A person who takes steps which will lead a person who acts in a particular way to conclude that his business is that of another is guilty of passing off just as much as a person who states that his business is that of another."

The defendants were ordered to install a pre-recorded explanatory message.

Member of association

5.25   See para. 2.14, *supra*.

E. LICENSING AND FRANCHISING

Introduction

5.26   The failure of the plaintiffs in *Harrods v. Harrodian School*[6] should not be taken as casting doubt on the proposition that a misrepresentation that one is the licensee of the plaintiff is potentially actionable as passing-off. Millett L.J. approved statements in *British Legion v. British Legion Club (Street)*[7] and *Bulmer v. Bollinger*[8] and identified the "gist of the matter" as being whether the plaintiffs would have been taken as having made themselves responsible for the quality of the defendants' goods or services. On the facts of *Harrods*, that was not made out. A mere belief that there was sponsorship or financial support, for instance, would be insufficient.

---

[4] [1995] R.P.C. 15 (Aldous J.).
[5] That the defendants intended to divert business.
[6] Court of Appeal, to be reported.
[7] (1931) 48 R.P.C. 555 (Farwell J.).
[8] [1972] F.S.R. 119; [1973] R.P.C. 439, C.A.

G. CHARACTER MERCHANDISING

Introduction

Nice and Safe Attitude v. Flook,[9] though not a character merchandising case, **5.40** is reminiscent of *Tavener Rutledge v. Trexapalm*[10] in that a licence from the American National Aeronautics and Space Administration to the defendant's suppliers for use on T-shirts did not justify varying an injunction granted in favour of the plaintiffs who had been the first in England to use a similar logo for clothing, though without having any connection with NASA (USA).

The return of South Africa to international sports provided the background to *FIFA v. Bartlett*[11] where better evidence allowed the *Dallas*[12] case to be distinguished. The defendant had had the foresight to register *World Cup* as a trade mark when sanctions were in force and there seemed to be no prospect of South Africa competing internationally. During the 1994 football World Cup in America he not only launched his own unlicensed range of sports clothing but demanded royalties (of $12 \frac{1}{2}$ per cent) from South Africa *FIFA* sponsors and licensees. As in *Mirage Studios v. Counter-Feat Clothing*,[13] which Joffe J. followed, this was a rare care of a defendant actually holding himself out as entitled to grant licences.

Character mechandising is not confined to the characters as such, but can extend to their props, which in the case of the television series The Simpsons included the imaginary brand of beer which was drunk by Homer Simpson and his friends. In *Twentieth Century Fox Film v. South Australia Brewing*[14] the producers of The Simpsons were granted an interlocutory injunction against a real brand of beer being launched as "Duff Beer" without their licence. They had consistently refused to grant licences in relation to alcoholic drinks.

A mild example of "ambush" marketing comes from New Zealand. In *New Zealand Olympic and Commonwealth Games Association v. Telecom New Zealand*[15] an advertisement which said that you could take the defendants' mobile phones to the (Atlanta) Olympics was unlikely to be taken as representing that the advisers was connected with or a sponsor of the Olympic Games. The device of using the word "RING" five times and in five colours in the manner of the Olympic symbol was more likely to cause amusement than confusion. There might be a marginally arguable case but the balance of convenience favoured the defendants.

---

[9] (Robert Walker J., February 8, 1996).
[10] [1975] F.S.R. 479; [1977] R.P.C. 275 (Walton J.).
[11] 1994 (4) SA 722 (Joffe J., TPD).
[12] *Lorimar Productions v. Sterling Clothing* [1982] R.P.C. 395 (Van Dijkhorst J., Transvaal).
[13] [1991] F.S.R. 145 (Browne-Wilkinson V.-C.).
[14] (1996) 34 I.P.R. 225 (Tamberlin J., Federal Court).
[15] [1996] F.S.R. 757 (McGechan J., High Court of New Zealand). The report at (1996) 35 I.P.R. 55 reproduces the advertisement.

The *Teenage Mutant Ninja Turtles* case

5.41 *Nice and Safe Attitude v. Flook*,[16] treats the *Teenage Mutant Ninja Turtles*[17] case as turning on copyright considerations.

I. INVERSE PASSING-OFF

Inverse passing-off in English law: *Bristol Conservatories*

5.55 Now that inverse passing-off is well accepted in principle, attention can turn to the situations in which there is a sufficiently material misrepresentation to create liability. In *Chater v. Rose*[18] the use of the slogan "It's Back" for the defendants' production of *Peter Pan* might have been passing-off, if it suggested that the defendants' pantomime in 1993 was the same as or associated with the plaintiffs' production of the pantomime at the same theatre in 1991, but the offending material was withdrawn and the point was not decided. In the Singapore case of *John Robert Powers School v. Tessensohn*,[19] the use of the plaintiffs' lecture notes at the defendants' self-development school amounted to inverse passing-off but statements in the defendants' literature to which the plaintiffs objected were "puffing" rather than an attempt to misappropriate credit properly due to the plaintiffs. In *Leec v. Morquip*[20] there was a conflict of evidence as to whether the defendants' use of photographs of the plaintiffs' mortuary equipment had been misleading or not. Laddie J. held that the plaintiffs had not discharged the burden of proof on them and found for the defendants.

J. CONCLUSION: A GENERAL RULE

The common principle

5.61 See para. 4.03 for *SDS Biotech v. Power*[21] and *Hodge Clemco v. Airblast*.[22]

---

[16] *Supra.*
[17] *Mirage Studios v. Counter-Feat Clothing Co Ltd* [1991] F.S.R. 145 (Browne-Wilkinson V.-C.).
[18] [1994] F.S.R. 491 (Jacob J.).
[19] [1995] F.S.R. 947 (C.A., Singapore).
[20] (Laddie J., February 16, 1996).
[21] (1989) [1995] F.S.R. 797 (Aldous J.).
[22] [1995] F.S.R. 806 (Jacob J.).

CHAPTER 6

INDICIA

A. DISTINCTIVENESS

Spontaneous public adoption

6.06 In *British Diabetic Association v. The Diabetic Society*[1] the plaintiffs failed to make out that *British Diabetic Society* and *Diabetic Society* were their "nicknames" in which they had a *de facto* exclusive reputation, but the defendants' name was confusingly similar to the plaintiffs' actual name and a final injunction was granted.

Mere association with plaintiff

6.07 In *Harrods v. Harrodian School*[2] Beldam L.J. would have been prepared to accept "that some members of the public would associate the respondents' enterprise [school] with the appellant." But, alluding to the words of Lord Oliver in *Reckitt & Colman v. Borden*,[3] any such confusion would be irrelevant: "To be actionable, the confusion caused must lead the public to believe that the goods or services offered by the defendant are the goods or services of the plaintiff and by reason of that erroneous belief in the public be likely to cause damage to the goodwill of the plaintiff's business."

B. ESTABLISHING DISTINCTIVENESS

Nature of use

6.10 Use of the term *Harrodian* in various contexts in which it did not come to the attention of the public did not assist the plaintiffs in *Harrods v. Harrodian School.*[4] Other examples of use were irrelevant as having been discontinued long ago.

Primary association not with plaintiff

6.13 *Harrods v. Harrodian School*[5] may be a case where confusion was more likely with Harrow School (whose pupils are *Harrovians*) than with the plaintiffs' department store.

Loss of distinctiveness

6.17 In *Harrods v. Harrodian School*,[6] the plaintiffs had at one time used *Harrodian* on a small range of disparate goods (clothes, chocolates, butter and

---

[1] [1996] F.S.R. 1 (Robert Walker J.). Citing *Heels v. Stafford Heels Ltd* (1927) 44 R.P.C. 299.
[2] Court of Appeal, to be reported.
[3] [1990] 1 W.L.R. 491; [1990] 1 All E.R. 873; [1990] R.P.C. 340 (H.L.).
[4] Court of Appeal, to be reported.
[5] *Supra.*
[6] *Supra.*

dog biscuits) but such use was irrelevant since they had long ago discontinued it. Proposals for a *Harrodian* bar, health club and cookery school would be "a revival of a use which the Plaintiffs used to make but which they have not for many years actually made."

C. ASSESSING THE PROBABILITY OF DECEPTION

The persons to consider

In *Neutrogena v. Golden*[7] it was common ground that the majority of **6.23** customers would not be confused by the defendants' *Neutralia* range, but the evidence showed that a substantial number of ordinary members of the public would be confused, and an injunction was granted at trial and upheld on appeal. It was best to avoid expressions such as "more than *de minimis*" which could give a misleading impression of the level of confusion required.

Defendant's goods or business distinguished

Distinctive packaging was insufficient to avoid liability for passing-off in **6.24** *Neutrogena v. Golden*[8] where the names *Neutrogena* and *Neutralia* were too similar.

D. DESCRIPTIVE AND GENERIC TERMS

Minor differences sufficient to distinguish

In *Jian Tools for Sales v. Roderick Manhattan Group*[9] Knox J. held that **6.33** *BizPlan Builder* for computer software was sufficiently fanciful for *BusinessPlan Builder* to be an inadequate distinction, at least for the purposes of an interlocutory injunction. It did not help the defendants that they had themselves applied to register *BusinessPlan Builder* as a service mark, implicitly asserting its distinctiveness. In *British Diabetic Association v. The Diabetic Society*[10] it was conceded that the plaintiff still had goodwill in relation to its previous name, *Diabetic Association*, even though it had been changed in 1954, so that the word *British* was not to be included in the comparison. On the facts, the name of the defendant charity was not sufficiently distinct and an injunction was granted.

---

[7] [1996] R.P.C. 473, C.A.
[8] [1996] R.P.C. 473, C.A.
[9] [1995] F.S.R. 924 (Knox J.).
[10] [1996] F.S.R. 1 (Robert Walker J.).

Whether used as trade mark by defendant or customer

6.34 Kettle had acquired secondary meaning in relation to crisps but was still sufficiently descriptive for use of the expression "Double Crunch Kettle Cooked Potato Chips" not to amount to passing-off, especially as the defendants' get-up was distinct: *Pepsico Australia v. Kettle Chip Co.*[11]

F. TITLES

Television and Radio

6.45 The producers of the *Baywatch* television series was refused an interlocutory injunction against satellite broadcasting of a series of erotic videos called *Babewatch* as there was no risk of confusion and the balance of convenience was against them.[12]

Plays and films

6.47 In *Chater v. Rose*[13] the use of the slogan "It's Back" for the defendants' production of *Peter Pan* might have been passing-off, if it suggested that the defendants' pantomime in 1993 was the same as or associated with the plaintiffs' production of the pantomime at the same theatre in 1991, but the offending material was withdrawn and the point was not decided. *Police America* for a video of real life American police car chases would have been protected but for the fact that the plaintiffs' video had not yet been launched or sufficiently publicised: *Labyrinth Media v. Brave World.*[14]

I. VISUAL MARKS AND ASPECTS OF GET-UP

Colour, shape and size

6.66 An allegation of passing-off based on imitation of the grey colour of the plaintiffs fungicide itself (not on the packaging, which was distinct) was just arguable and would not be struck out: *SDS Biotech v. Power.*[15]

---

[11] (1996) 33 I.P.R. 161 (Federal Court).
[12] *Baywatch Production Co. Ltd v. The Home Video Channel* (Michael Crystal Q.C., Deputy Judge, July 31, 1996).
[13] [1994] F.S.R. 491 (Jacob J.).
[14] [1995] EMLR 38 (Blackburne J.).
[15] (1989) [1995] F.S.R. 797 (Aldous J.).

Colour and shape of bottles and containers

The defendants' tins of lighter fuel were fraudulently got up to deceive in the **6.67** Chinese market in *Modus Vivendi (Ronson) v. Keen*.[16]

J. MISCELLANIA

Numerals, part numbers, telephone numbers

In *Law Society v. Griffiths*[17] the plaintiffs were awarded an interlocutory **6.70** injunction to protect their "Accident Line"—an accident and personal injury advice and referral scheme using the telephone number 0500 192939—against the use by the defendant firm of solicitors of the number 0800 192939. The injunction in terms prevented the defendants from answering the 0800 number except by way of a corrective pre-recorded message and ordered them to procure British Telecom to re-direct calls from the 0800 number to the Law Society's 0500 number.

In a New Zealand case, *Glev v. Foodmakers*,[18] the plaintiffs were an Australian chain of Pizza outlets trading as *Pizza Haven* which all used telephone numbers terminating in 241, to advertise their marketing policy of two pizze for the price of one. In New Zealand the number used for all seven recently opened branches was 0800 831 241. They were granted an interlocutory injunction against another pizza outlet using 0800 241 241.

[16] (Lightman J., July 5, 1995).
[17] [1995] R.P.C. 16 (Aldous J.).
[18] (1996) 33 I.P.R. 550 (Blanchard J., High Court of New Zealand).

DEFENCES

A. ILLEGAL OR DECEPTIVE MARK OR TRADE

The basis and effect of the doctrine

7.01 Damages were awarded in *Modus Vivendi (Ronson) v. Keen*[1] despite the fact that the plaintiffs had systematically and dishonestly exaggerated the contents of their tins of lighter fuel. Lightman J. disapproved of the plaintiffs' conduct in this respect but the defendants were fraudulent, equitable relief was not sought, and the defence does not seem to have been raised as such.

D. CONCURRENT AND ANTECEDENT RIGHTS

Antecedent rights

7.18 In *Law Society v. Griffiths*[2] the defendants were restrained from using the telephone number 0800 192939 although their use narrowly anticipated that of

[1] (Lightman J., July 5, 1995).
[2] [1995] R.P.C. 16 (Aldous J.).

the plaintiffs' number 0500 192939. One way of understanding the decision would be to say that the injunction was essentially *quia timet* and that the defendants' actual use—being unpublicised, colourable and in dubious faith—was insufficient to give rise to any defence of antecedent user.

F. EUROPEAN COMMUNITY LAW

Introduction

The argument based on Community law proposed by Graham J. in *Maxim's v.* **7.24**
Dye,[3] which is criticised in the main work, received a clear, though implicit, repudiation in the judgment of Aldous J. in *British Sky Broadcasting v. David Lyons*[4] where the defendant argued that the plaintiffs' statutory transmission rights could not be enforced because the UK legislation conferred such rights only in respect of transmissions originating in the United Kingdom. In rejecting this submission, Aldous J. drew an analogy with passing-off:

> "Similarly, the right to restrain passing off is only available to traders with goodwill in the United Kingdom. Thus the condition for obtaining the right to restrain passing off is local trade, but that does not amount to illegal discrimination or a disguised restriction on trade between member states."

---

[3] [1977] 1 W.L.R. 1155; [1978] 2 All E.R. 55; [1977] F.S.R. 364 (Graham J.).
[4] [1995] F.S.R. 357 (Aldous J.).

ENFORCEMENT

A. INTERLOCUTORY REMEDIES

Discovery of infringers' identity

In *Coca Cola Company and Schweppes v. Gilbey*[1] the defendant was ordered   **8.03**
to comply with an order to disclose the identities of others involved in large
scale counterfeiting, despite a fear of violence towards himself.

Procedure on interlocutory motions

Labyrinth Media v. Brave World[2] confirms that the opposite party should   **8.04**
normally be notified of an intended *ex parte* application. *Anton Piller* orders
and *Mareva* injunctions were recognised as exceptions to this principle but
even an apparently justified suspicion that the defendants were trying to steal
a march on the plaintiffs in the market was not a sufficient reason for failing
to put the defendants on notice. The *ex parte* injunction was discharged for
other reasons and an enquiry as to damages on the cross-undertaking was
ordered.

In *Labyrinth Media v. Brave World (No 2)*[3] the plaintiffs were refused an
adjournment of their *inter partes* motion after an *ex parte* motion had been
discharged for lack of evidence of reputation and goodwill and there was no
more than a hope that that such evidence would be forthcoming. They would
not be precluded from bringing a new motion on new evidence, but it was an
abuse of process to allow the motion to remain in existence in the meantime.
The *inter partes* motion was therefore dismissed.

C. INTERLOCUTORY INJUNCTIONS AND AMERICAN CYANAMID

Express derogations from *Cyanamid*

In *Series 5 Software v. Clarke*,[4] a breach of confidence case, Laddie J.   **8.17**
suggested that notwithstanding *American Cyanamid* it was proper, in a
sufficiently clear case, to take the strength or weakness of the plaintiff's case
on the merits into account alongside the balance of convenience. *Series 5* has
not been followed by other judges, but the blurring of issues which occurs in
passing-off means that it would not make that much difference in practice.

---

[1] [1996] F.S.R. 23 (Lightman J.).
[2] [1995] EMLR 38 (Blackburne J.).
[3] [1995] EMLR 50 (Blackburne J.).
[4] [1996] F.S.R. 273 (Laddie J.).

D. THE BALANCE OF CONVENIENCE

Are damages adequate reparation?

8.21 The prospect of the distinctiveness of the plaintiffs' exclusive *Xeryus* brand of men's fragrances being swamped by the defendants' down-market *Xereux* brand with no prospect of the situation being restored after trial was the main reason for granting an interlocutory injunction in *Parfums Givenchy v. Designer Alternatives*.[5]

Order of magnitude and ability to pay

8.23 Security of £62,500 to support the cross-undertaking was ordered in *Jian Tools for Sales v. Roderick Manhattan Group*.[6]

E. THE OTHER ISSUES ON MOTION

The status quo

8.26 Lord Diplock's speech in *Garden Cottage v. Milk Marketing Board*[7] was interpreted by Knox J. in *Jian Tools for Sales v. Roderick Manhattan Group*[8] as meaning that Lord Diplock's treatment of delay was not to be taken as referring only to any unreasonable delay between issue of the writ and service of the notice of motion. However, the plaintiffs had not delayed unduly and the relevant date for determining the status quo was in mid-April, when the defendants entered the market, rather than at the end of May when the writ was issued. The status quo therefore favoured the grant of an injunction.

Delay

8.28 In *BASF v. CEP*[9] delay in suing between late March and mid-July was not adequately explained and was one reason for refusing an interlocutory injunction. Six weeks' delay after the defendants entered the market was not fatal in *Jian Tools for Sales v. Roderick Manhattan Group*[10] and any delay before that point could not be criticised.

---

[5] [1994] R.P.C. 243, C.A. Passing-off was alleged but the case was argued solely as one of trade mark infringement.
[6] [1995] F.S.R. 924 (Knox J.). Costs were separately provided for.
[7] [1984] 1 A.C. 130 (H.L.).
[8] [1995] F.S.R. 924 (Knox J.).
[9] (Knox J., October 26, 1995).
[10] [1995] F.S.R. 924 (Knox J.).

Special factors and discretion

One reason for granting an interlocutory injunction in *Law Society v.* **8.29**
Griffiths[11] was that it was not in the public interest for very similar telephone
numbers to be used by both parties: one for an independent accident referral
service and the other for a single solicitors' practice. In *Law Society v. Society
of Lawyers*[12] the public interest also strongly favoured the grant of an
interlocutory injunction since the public would be misled about the nature and
status of the defendant and the qualifications it purported to grant. The
defendant was not a professional association of lawyers in any real sense, its
members did not have to be legally qualified and were not subject to any
objective entrance requirements or discipline.

F. PROCEDURE

Representative actions

See para. 2.14, *supra*. **8.35**

Summary judgment

Brain v. Ingledew Brown Bennison and Garret,[13] though a threats action in the **8.38**
Patents Court, is of interest as demonstrating the limitations of R.S.C., Ord.
14A in dealing with the sort of mixed questions of fact and law equally typical
in passing-off.

G. EVIDENCE: GENERAL PRINCIPLES

Trade and retail evidence

As in patent law, it has tended to be assumed in passing-off that the "ultimate **8.41**
issue" rule still exists, even if it is not always observed. For the contrary
possibility see *infra* at para. 8.45.

Trade evidence—examples

Trade evidence of likely confusion (as opposed to opinion evidence from **8.43**
members of the public) was treated as admissible and relevant by Knox J. in

---

[11] [1995] R.P.C. 16 (Aldous J.).
[12] [1996] F.S.R. 739 (Rimer J.).
[13] [1996] F.S.R. 341 (C.A.).

Jian Tools for Sales v. Roderick Manhattan Group[14] where the market was for computer software for generating business plans. In *Neutrogena v. Golden*[15] the evidence of shopkeepers that they had not observed confusion between *Neutrogena* and *Neutralia* and were willing to stock the two side by side was allowed to be relevant but given little weight by Jacob J. or the Court of Appeal: shopkeepers would not be aware of the sort of confusion otherwise proved to exist and the name was not self-evidently deceptive. Expert evidence on brand-switching by a professor of marketing was admitted, but given no weight.

Consumer evidence, actual deception and trap orders

8.44 The general principle was stated by Millett L.J. in *Harrods v. Harrodian School*[16] as follows:

> "Evidence of actual confusion is always relevant and may be decisive. Absence of such evidence may often be readily explained and is rarely decisive. Its weight is a matter for the judge."

The absence of evidence of actual confusion was regarded as "compelling" by Harman J. at trial, and as "not without significance" by Millett L.J. in the Court of Appeal. The defendant school had been announced in February 1993, opened in September 1993 with 70 pupils and the trial was in May 1994, a timetable which hardly gave much opportunity for any such evidence to come to light unless the victims of confusion recovered from it quickly and actually came forward to volunteer themselves as witnesses. The dissenting judgment of Sir Michael Kerr expresses the same principle as Millett L.J. but is more realistic in this respect:

> "Even if there is no evidence of confusion whatever, the court must decide for itself, and may conclude that passing-off has been established: see e.g. per Sir Raymond Evershed M.R. in *Electrolux Ltd v. Electrix Ltd* (1953) 71 RPC 23 (CA) at p. 31. Thus, it has often been said that the availability of such evidence is important, but not its absence, because it is notoriously difficult to procure such evidence. In the present case, given the recency of the start-up of the school, this is even less surprising."

The evidence of two local residents who thought that the presence of a sign in *Harrods* livery then remaining at the site meant that the site of the school was owned by Harrods was rightly dismissed by the majority as worthless.

In *BASF v. CEP*[17] the evidence of farmers that their first reaction on seeing *Farming Opus* for a trade directory was to assume a connection with the

[14] [1995] F.S.R. 924 (Knox J.).
[15] [1996] R.P.C. 473, C.A. *affirming* Jacob J. *ibid.*
[16] Court of Appeal, to be reported.
[17] (Knox J., October 26, 1995).

plaintiffs' *Opus* brand of pesticide was of very little value. Anyone looking beyond the cover would not be confused.

Several categories of consumer and trade evidence were examined in *Neutrogena v. Golden.*[18] The case was a marginal one on first impression and consumer evidence was crucial. As Jacob J. put it:

> "If the judge's own opinion is that the case is marginal, one where he cannot be sure whether there is a likelihood of sufficient deception, the case will fail in the absence of enough evidence of the likelihood of deception. But if that opinion of the judge is supplemented by such evidence then it will succeed. And even if one's own opinion is that deception is unlikely though possible, convincing evidence of deception will carry the day. . . . It was certainly my experience in practice that my own view as to the likelihood of deception was not always reliable. As I grew more experienced I said more and more 'it depends on the evidence'."

The plaintiffs relied on several categories of consumer evidence. First, a television advertisement for *Neutralia*, showing a woman's bare nipple, had produced numerous complaints to the Independent Television Commission, some of them attributing the advertisement to *Neutrogena*. Secondly, there were members of the public who had communicated with the plaintiffs or defendants, including one who had bought *Neutralia* in the belief it was made by *Neutrogena*. An e-mail message around the plaintiffs' solicitors asking if anyone had bought or used *Neutralia* products produced instances of confusion; and finally a "witness collection programme" at chemists' shops produced 11 members of the public who gave evidence in person or by witness statement, as did some of the interviewers. Attacks on the inferences drawn from all these categories of evidence failed on appeal.

H. SURVEY EVIDENCE

Introduction

The "witness collection programme" in *Neutrogena v. Golden*[19] was not a **8.45** survey in the normal sense, and it was not relied on its totality to show what proportion of customers would be confused. Although the plaintiffs were ordered to produce all their questionnaires, they offered no expert statistical analysis. The purpose was simply to identify suitable witnesses who were called for cross-examination, a procedure of which Jacob J. approved[20]:

---

[18] [1996] R.P.C. 473, C.A. *affirming* Jacob J. *ibid.*

[19] [1996] R.P.C. 473, C.A. *affirming* Jacob J. *ibid.*

[20] [1996] R.P.C. 473, Jacob J. *affirmed*, C.A. *ibid.* Three routine surveys by the defendants were also regarded as relevant in the Court of Appeal.

"This was rather different from an ordinary market survey of the kind which has sometimes been before the courts. In a normal market survey the members of the public are interviewed according to a set pattern of questions and their answers recorded on forms. The answers are classified according to a code and then analysed. Often statisticians come along and give evidence, based upon collation of data from surveys as to the statistical validity of conclusions. The evidence often contains long explanations from statisticians of things like 'confidence limits.' I have long thought that sort of exercise as such is unnecessarily elaborate in a passing off action. The court in a passing off case is not concerned with statistical precision. What it wants to know is whether or not there is a substantial degree of deception or confusion. Moreover pure questionnaire evidence is seldom helpful—there are almost inevitable faults with the questions or the recordal of the answers as well as in later stages of the processing. Of course the court needs to know how the evidence was collected, and needs to have the full picture, including particularly what failed surveys, if any, there were. But unless one can have some real evidence, tested in cross-examination, one cannot really be sure of what was passing through people's minds. Those cases where surveys have proved to be useful have all involved some of the 'pollees' coming to court."

An informal telephone survey without expert statistical analysis was also conducted for the plaintiffs in *Wagamama v. City Centre Restaurants*[21] and some respondents gave oral evidence.

The main work suggests that a more fundamental objection to survey evidence than the hearsay rule is that the expert interpreting the survey is frequently asked to give opinion evidence on one of the ultimate issues in the action. Against this view, there is a school of thought represented by the Court of Appeal decision in the patent case of *Glaverbel v. British Coal Corp*[22] holding that since the coming into force of the Civil Evidence Act 1972, section 3, there is no longer any rule of law that an expert witness cannot give opinion evidence even on the very issue the court has to decide. The point has not been conclusively resolved either way.

The analogy between survey evidence and experiments in a patent action was applied by Jacob J. in the opposite direction in *Honeywell v. Appliance Components*,[23] where he suggested that, as with surveys, the experiments performed by a party in a patent infringement action should be disclosed in their entirety, if any of them were to be relied on. This interprets *Raffles* as meaning that preparatory or exploratory surveys—"failed surveys" in the language of *Neutrogena v. Golden*—do have to be disclosed, even if their purpose is essentially to test or refine the survey methodology.

---

[21] [1995] F.S.R. 713 (Laddie J.).
[22] [1995] R.P.C. 255; [1995] F.S.R. 254, C.A.
[23] (Jacob J., February 22, 1996).

The Civil Evidence Act 1995

The Civil Evidence Act 1995, when it comes into force, will abolish the **8.45/A** common law rule against the admission of hearsay evidence in civil proceedings and supersede the hearsay provisions of 1968 and 1972 Acts referred to in the main work. Section 1 provides:

(1) In civil proceedings evidence shall not be excluded on the ground that it is hearsay.

(2) In this Act—
 (a) "hearsay" means a statement made otherwise than by a person while giving oral evidence in the proceedings which is tendered as evidence of the matters stated; and
 (b) references to hearsay include hearsay of whatever degree.

(3) Nothing in this Act affects the admissibility of evidence admissible apart from this section.

(4) The provisions of sections 2 to 6 (safeguards and supplementary provisions relating to hearsay evidence) do not apply in relation to hearsay evidence admissible apart from this section, notwithstanding that it may also be admissible by virtue of this section.

Supplementary provisions require advance written notice of proposed hearsay evidence to be given, much as at present[24] and provide for the giver of the evidence to be called and cross-examined by the opposite party if necessary.[25]

Section 4 lists a number of factors the court is to take into account in estimating the weight to be given to hearsay:

4.(1) In estimating the weight (if any) to be given to hearsay evidence in civil proceedings the court shall have regard to any circumstances from which any inference can reasonably be drawn as to the reliability or otherwise of the evidence.

(2) Regard may be had, in particular, to the following—
 (a) whether it would have been reasonable and practicable for the party by whom the evidence was adduced to have produced the maker of the original statement as a witness;
 (b) whether the original statement was made contemporaneously with the occurrence or existence of the matters stated;
 (c) whether the evidence involves multiple hearsay;
 (d) whether any person involved had any motive to conceal or misrepresent matters;

---

[24] Section 2, the practical effect of which will depend on implementing Rules of Court which have yet to be made.
[25] Section 3.

(e) whether the original statement was an edited account, or was made in collaboration with another or for a particular purpose;

(f) whether the circumstances in which the evidence is adduced as hearsay are such as to suggest an attempt to prevent proper evaluation of its weight.

The transitional provisions for the Act, and in particular whether it will apply to hearsay evidence in existing proceedings, are to be made by Rules of Court.

Admissibility under the Civil Evidence Acts

8.48 See the commentary on the Civil Evidence Act 1995, *supra*.

Conduct of the survey: the *Raffles* criteria and other issues

8.49 Even if the survey is not relied upon as such, the *Raffles* criteria may still be applicable in part, as in *Neutrogena v. Golden*[26] where the plaintiffs were ordered to disclose all their questionnaires. A small field survey of farmers in *BASF v. CEP*[27] was criticised for falling into every trap the *Raffles* criteria were intended to avoid.

I. FINAL REMEDIES

Injunctions and declarations

8.51 Mandatory injunctions requiring a change of name are more readily given now than previously, even at the interlocutory stage, in comparison to the old and convoluted practice of granting a prohibitory injunction against the defendant continuing to exist under the disputed name. The defendant charity was ordered to change its name after trial in *British Diabetic Association v. Diabetic Society.*[28] In *Glaxo v. Glaxowellcome*[29] Lightman J. granted interlocutory mandatory injunctions requiring the defendant company and its promoters to change its name, but the reasoning is not entirely satisfactory. Rimer J. also made an interlocutory order for the defendant to change its name in *Law Society v. Society of Lawyers.*[30]

---

[26] [1996] R.P.C. 473, C.A.
[27] (Knox J., October 26, 1996).
[28] [1996] F.S.R. 1 (Robert Walker J.).
[29] [1996] F.S.R. 388 (Lightman J.).
[30] [1996] F.S.R. 739 (Rimer J.)

Corrective statements and apologies

In *Law Society v. Griffiths*[31] the defendants were ordered not to answer their **8.52** telephone number 0800 192939 except by way of a pre-recorded message stating that theirs was not the Law Society Accident Line which was available on 0500 192939. They were also ordered to procure British Telecom to re-direct calls from the 0800 number to the Law Society's 0500 number.

---

[31] [1995] R.P.C. 16 (Aldous J.).

INDEX